Age 7-9

NC Level 2
Scottish Level B

Extra Help
in
Maths

Practical special needs support

Rose Griffiths

acknowledgements

The author and publisher thank Cas Beckett for word-processing the original manuscript.

For the use of the contents pages from *How to Handle your Cat* by Roy Apps Text © 2001, Roy Apps; Illustration © 2001, Jo Moore (2001, Hippo)

For the National Numeracy Strategy *Framework for Teaching Mathematics* © Crown copyright. Reproduced under the terms of HMSO Guidance Note 8.

For the National Curriculum for mathematics © Crown copyright. Material is reproduced with the permission of the Controller of HMSO and the Queen's Printer for Scotland.

For the Scottish National Guidelines for Mathematics 5–14 © Crown copyright. Material is reproduced with the permission of the Controller of HMSO and the Queen's Printer for Scotland.

Every effort has been made to trace the copyright holders and the publisher apologises for any errors or omissions.

author
Rose Griffiths

editor
Irene Goodacre

assistant editors
Nina Bruges
Jon Hill

photography
Martyn F Chillmaid

series designer
Heather C Sanneh

designer
Heather C Sanneh

illustrations
Teri Gower/Malcolm Sherman

cover image
Getty images/Romilly Lockyer

Text © Rose Griffiths 2004
© 2004 Scholastic Ltd

Designed using Adobe InDesign™

Published by Scholastic Ltd,
Villiers House,
Clarendon Avenue,
Leamington Spa,
Warwickshire CV32 5PR

Printed by Belmont Press, Northampton

1 2 3 4 5 6 7 8 9 0   4 5 6 7 8 9 0 1 2 3

British Library Cataloguing-in-Publication Data
A catalogue record for this book is available from the British Library.

ISBN 0-439-97108-X
Visit our website at www.scholastic.co.uk

acknowledgements

contents

Using
this **book**

This book has been written primarily for teachers and classroom assistants working in mainstream schools, who are looking for ways of helping children in the lowest 20% of the attainment range. Parents will also find plenty of activities here that they can share and enjoy with their children, to give them extra help in maths.

Organisation

The ideas are especially for those children who need more examples and more practice than others, to understand and remember each new mathematical concept.

This book includes four different sections of information:
● general advice about ways of working (pages 5–9);
● background mathematical information about:
  Number (pages 10–11),
  Calculations (pages 26–27) and
  Measures, shape and space (pages 46–47);
● double-page spreads of notes, ideas and illustrations to support particular mathematical topics;
● summary of objectives (pages 62–64).

Topic spreads

Each spread includes:
● notes on teaching and learning for that specific topic, to help with setting clear objectives for the work;
● examples of activities that children have enjoyed and found useful. These are explained briefly so that you can tailor them for use in any teaching situation: for example, as the main activity for a group of children in a whole-class lesson, or for a pair of children to do, working with additional adult help.

Photocopiable sheets

Some activities are supported by photocopiable pages that can be found on pages 52–61. These can be photocopied for use in school or at home. Colour copies are especially attractive to children, but black and white copies will also work well.

Summary of objectives

The main teaching objectives for each topic are summarised on pages 62–64. Pages 62–63 provide the relevant information for England while page 64 covers the curriculum for Scotland.

Planning
for **success**

Learning mathematics is not always straightforward, and children do not always learn at a steady rate. However, even at the age of only five or six, some children's slower progress in maths may be a cause for concern. By the time a child is seven, eight or nine, they may be convinced that they are 'hopeless' at maths, and give up trying to learn altogether.

Fortunately, there are many ways in which low-attaining children can be helped to understand, remember and use mathematics more successfully. Many of the principles involved are valuable for children at all levels of attainment.

© JAMES LEVIN/SODA

Practical activities are fun – and can show children how maths is used in everyday life

Causes of low attainment

The causes of children's low attainment in maths are very varied. Sometimes, with young children, it is simply lack of experience. Sometimes difficulties stem from the same problems that make it hard for children to make a confident start to reading (and this might include specific learning difficulties, or more general problems with concentration, memory, or processing language). Some children's problems arise because they have been 'moved on' to new work before they sufficiently understood the previous underlying concepts; children who have changed school or missed school may have significant gaps in their knowledge. Some children have physical or sensory difficulties. Whatever the cause of a child's slow progress, there is always something you can do to help.

How to help

What are the best ways of helping children succeed? Here are some general principles to think about.

• **Show that maths is useful and enjoyable**
Maths *must* make sense to children. We need to make the most of children's own interests and experience at home and in school, to show them where and how maths is used. High motivation to learn is particularly important for those who find learning difficult, so enjoyment and a clear purpose are doubly important for low-attaining children.

• **Build confidence**
Unfortunately, sometimes children's previous experience of learning maths has been so unsuccessful that they lack the confidence needed

© CREATAS

**Practising skills with a partner is
an excellent way to build confidence**

introduction

to make good progress. The fear of getting things
wrong can make some children feel so anxious
that they put all their energies into avoiding work,
using tactics ranging from spending a long time
sharpening their pencils, to being naughty.

How can you give children fresh hope that it might
be worth trying again? It can be helpful to tell
children that some parts of maths can be quite hard
to explain, so it is not surprising that people don't
always understand them first time. It is also worth
emphasising that mistakes in maths can be very
useful because they help point out something new
you can learn. This is much better than *accidentally*
getting something right, because then you don't
find out that you didn't really understand it.

Working with a partner is useful in lots of ways,
but can especially help build confidence as children
practise explaining things to each other, comparing
answers, and making up questions for each other.

When children are particularly stuck on one aspect
of maths, it will often be more effective to switch
to a different area of work for a while – ideally, one

where success is guaranteed! Returning to a difficult
idea after a breathing space is more helpful than a
long stretch of failure.

• Encourage children to be independent
Children whose attainment in maths is low will often
benefit from additional adult support. However, it
is crucial to achieve an effective balance – providing
the level of support children need to help them learn
quickly and confidently, without giving so much help
that they really haven't done any work themselves.
Progress is not about leading children through a series
of steps to the right answer; it is about helping them to
the point where they are able to think for themselves
about how they are going to solve a problem.

Discuss the pace of learning with children. Explain
that you want them to learn as much as they can,
so you don't want to go too slowly; but that you
also don't want to go so fast that they haven't got
time to understand new ideas. Encourage children
to ask questions, to think about things they could do
that would help them learn more, and to take joint
responsibility with you for making the most of their
time. Children can often help set short-term tasks

or targets for themselves. For example: *'I'll practise counting in twos for five minutes every day this week'* or *'I'll learn how to spell* triangle *by Friday.'*

Use activities with a simple method of work, but which can be repeated with different equipment, or in a different order, or with other slight variations. Try to provide enough variety to hold children's interest, but without so many changes that you spend too much time explaining what to do.

Problems with reading can sometimes hold children back, compared to their peers. Two strategies are particularly useful:
• Look for ways of making the ability to read less necessary (by using aural and practical work, for example).

• Teach reading alongside maths (making the most of opportunities to use written maths material as non-fiction texts for reading, writing and spelling).

• **Use varied teaching approaches**
It is important to use a variety of teaching approaches to improve the chances of finding effective ways of working with each child. Variety can also help children concentrate for longer on a particular topic, and using two or three complementary ways of working to solve a problem can increase children's understanding of what they are doing. Within any individual teaching session, look for ways of using all the child's available senses, and encouraging them to be active learners.

A full repertoire of work in maths for children aged seven to nine is likely to include practical work, role play, discussion and demonstration, using games and number equipment, and mental methods. It is also likely to include using resources such as calculators, computers, videos, audio tapes and books. Sometimes children will work on their own; more often, they should work with a partner, in a group, or with the whole class.

Some children will have more significant difficulties and will have an Individual Education Plan (IEP) that results in their working towards the same objective for many lessons. In such cases, teaching variety is critical to maintaining the child's motivation and increasing the chances of finding a key to his or her understanding.

Different resources can be employed to support different teaching approaches

© JAMES LEVIN/SODA

Extra Help in **Maths**
Ages 7–9 NC Level 2 Scottish Level B

7

introduction

● **Link assessment and teaching**

Every child learns best when their teacher has clear objectives for teaching and learning. You need to match your objectives to what the child already knows and understands, and you need to have realistic but high expectations of how to build on that. However, it is not easy to find out what someone already knows and understands in maths, especially with pupils who are convinced they can't do anything!

Often, the best way of assessing a child's understanding is to give them a problem to solve or an activity to do, and to watch them and discuss their work with them. Whatever form of assessment you use, it is important to explain to the child what you want to achieve: *'I want to find out how much you already know about this so that we can decide what you need to do next.'* With low-attaining children, assessment needs to be done very thoughtfully, so that they are convinced it is helpful, not humiliating.

Children whose progress is slow or erratic do need reassurance that they really are making progress. You may want to consider repeating an assessment activity after a gap of a few weeks, to show children that they can do more now than they could a little while ago.

● **Make the most of every possible opportunity to learn**

Maths learning does not happen exclusively in maths lessons, of course, and children who need

extra time to think about new ideas, or to practise skills, can gain from making the most of mathematical elements right across the curriculum, throughout the school day, and at home. Quite small things can prove significant – the chance to play a game again with a parent or carer at home, or a display in the corridor where a child queues up to go in for lunch. Never underestimate the power of incidental learning!

It can also be very valuable to look for ways of providing additional short 'teaching slots'. Allow five or ten minutes outside the usual time allocated for maths, when children can work with a partner or an adult on an activity already tried in a main lesson, or do some preparatory work to increase their chances of participating well in the next whole-class lesson.

● **Use sensible strategies for differentiation**

Differentiation is used to make sure that children at different levels of attainment all have access to work pitched at a suitable level: not so easy that it is boring, nor so challenging that it is impossible.

Children aged seven to nine change extremely fast, and learn at very different rates, partly depending on previous experience. It is important to avoid putting artificial limits on their learning, either through the tasks you give them or through the way you organise your class into groups. If children are put into attainment groups, it is important to review those groups frequently, and to use them flexibly.

Use open-ended tasks as often as possible – those where children all work on the same investigation or activity, but at their own level, with resulting work at their own level of achievement. This is known as 'differentiation by outcome'.

Work on shape and space (and sometimes measures) is often more accessible to children of all levels of attainment. Number, however, is more hierarchical, so there is more need to consider 'differentiation by task'. This involves providing separate activities

18 19 20 21 22 23 24 25 26 27 28

Brief additional adult help carefully for effective differentiation support

for children at different levels of attainment (and sometimes a choice of equipment to use, to help children tackle an activity that would otherwise be too difficult).

You can sometimes differentiate by providing additional adult support. This will always be more effective if the adult knows not just what activity to do with the child or group of children, but what it is hoped the children will learn.

In whole-class lessons, some children may need particular kinds of help for introductory and plenary sessions, where children from the whole range of attainment are participating. Sitting close to the teacher, in a position where they do not have to talk across the entire class to answer the teacher's questions, can help children feel more comfortable. A few minutes spent discussing 'what we are going to learn in our next lesson' shortly before the lesson can improve children's confidence and concentration (in much the same way that reading the 'blurb' on the back of a book

© KEN KARP AND STANLEL BACH/SODA

helps adults engage with a novel). Children may contribute to a plenary session more successfully if they are able to rehearse what they would say or show with another child or small group during the main part of the lesson.

Encourage and help all children to contribute to the plenary session

Down came the rain and
Washed the spider out.
Out came the sun and
Dried up all the rain.
And the eentsy weentsy spider
Went up the spout again.

© JAMES LEVIN/SODA

Extra help
with **number**

This book concentrates on building the skills and understanding of children who can already count up to about ten objects confidently, and who have made a start on simple practical and mental arithmetic with small numbers.

For more detailed information about earlier work, please see *Extra Help in Maths: Ages 5–7 (NC Level 1, Scottish Level A).*

Counting practice

For many low-attaining children, arithmetic starts to go wrong when they are asked to work with numbers that are bigger than the largest number they can count accurately. Regular counting practice is often the first and most important step in helping a low-attaining pupil to improve.

Children need experience of counting larger and larger numbers to help them develop a strong 'feel' for the size of numbers, and an understanding of how our number system counts in ones, tens, hundreds, and so on. This then makes them more confident and capable when they add, subtract, multiply and divide. Counting is the basis of arithmetic, and it is important that children have opportunities to practise counting, using bigger numbers as they gain in confidence, right to the end of primary school.

At the earliest stages, there are four important aspects of learning to count. The first three are: **knowing the number names; using one-to-one correspondence** (we count one number to each thing we are counting, without missing any out, and without counting anything twice); and **cardinality** (which means that the answer to a *How many?* question is the last number counted – the answer is 'Three', not 'One, two, three').

The fourth aspect of counting is one that develops gradually, as children's counting becomes more accurate: **conservation (or invariance) of number.**

© DIGITAL VISION LTD

This term is used to describe the fact that the number of objects in a group does not change, as long as none is added or taken away. To an adult this may seem obvious, but children often have doubts. Imagine you are not very good at counting: the first time you count a group of toy cars, you make it five; but the next time, there seem to be six. It isn't unreasonable for the child to think that the number can change.

© DAVID MAGER/SODA

Counting to 100

Once children *can* count small groups of objects accurately, which aspects of counting should you focus on for between ten and a hundred objects? Three things are important:

• Children need to learn and practise the **number names** from eleven to twenty, and the 'tens' numbers – thirty, forty, fifty and so on.

• By this stage, children should realise they must count one number to each object (**one-to-one correspondence**), but they may need help to manage this accurately and consistently. Show them how to move things out of the way as they count, putting them in a line, or grouping them in tens.

• If children exhibit a lack of accuracy when counting larger groups, this may mean that even though they have grasped the concept of conservation for smaller numbers, they still believe that bigger numbers can change. Further experience of accurate counting should convince them.

Counting practice can be linked with practice at reading numbers. Ask children to find the correct number from a set of cards to show what they have counted, or give them a number card to show how many things you want them to count. Encourage clear handwriting by providing purposeful contexts for good writing, such as writing questions for a friend to try. See pages 12 to 25 for further information and activities.

The ability to count a particular number of objects accurately (and to have done so often enough to be convinced that the number does stay the same) gives a solid foundation to number work within that **total. For example,** once a child can consistently **count a group of t**wenty objects accurately, he or **she can begin to w**ork on practical problems using **addition and subtr**action in everyday contexts within **a total of twenty.**

See 'Extra help with calculations' on pages 26–27 for further information.

Extra Help in **Maths**
Ages 7–9 NC Level 2 Scottish Level B

11

Counting games

Counting practice needs to be frequent and varied, particularly for older children who are not yet confident when counting 20 objects.

When children are still practising counting numbers of objects below 20, it is very important to check their accuracy as often as possible. Encourage them to move things as they count them, to avoid missing any out or counting any twice. Some children may be uncertain of the number names: '*eighteen, nineteen, tenteen…*' and will need reassurance, especially as they 'cross the tens', moving from 19 to 20, 29 to 30, and so on.

If children work with a partner, they can check (and so support) each other's work. This provides each child with extra counting practice, but in a different role. Children can also be responsible for deciding which numbers they should practise counting. They will often be more ambitious than you would expect.

Counting games and activities are more effective if they are co-operative rather than competitive, because it is easier to encourage children to help each other.

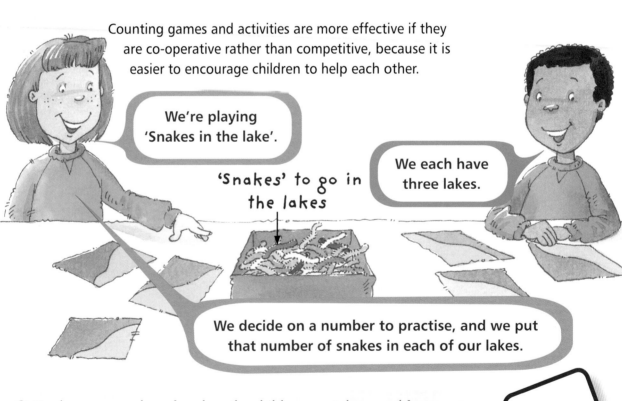

We're playing 'Snakes in the lake'.

'Snakes' to go in the lakes

We each have three lakes.

We decide on a number to practise, and we put that number of snakes in each of our lakes.

- To choose a number of snakes, the children can take a card from a set of 0 to 20 number cards, or just agree a number between themselves.

- When they have finished counting the snakes in their own lakes, each child checks the snakes in their partner's lakes. (This means each child has counted the practice number six times.)

- Put the snakes back. Choose a new number to practise.

Each game shown here can be used in the same way, so you can provide variety without having to give new explanations of what to do. Each game uses six 'boards' and up to about 120 'counters'. (Similar games, which are good for working with smaller numbers, are described in *Extra Help in Maths: Ages 5–7, NC Level 1*.)

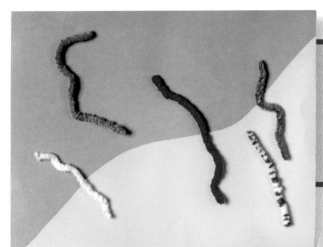

Snakes in the lake

Cut out six rectangles of blue card (about A5 size). Stick on yellow felt or sticky paper to make a sandy shoreline on each one. Cut pieces of pipe-cleaner to be the snakes.

People on the bus

Photocopy page 52 onto card three times to make six bus cards. To make people, draw faces on dried butter beans with permanent pens.

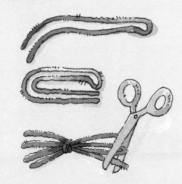

Spiders on webs

Photocopy page 53 onto card three times to make six spiders' web cards.

Make spiders by cutting 40cm lengths of wool or thin string. Fold each length in half, then in half again. Tie a knot in the middle, then cut off the ends.

Further ideas for using these games are on pages 28 and 29.

Counting library

Children need regular counting practice to help them make progress in understanding the number system. Children are more likely to try to count accurately when they use items they find attractive, because they will be interested to know how many there are.

Variety is important too. Not all children will like the same things, and they can also concentrate for longer if they are able to repeat an activity using different equipment. Work with the children to create a collection or 'library' of a wide variety of items that are suitable for counting. This should be organised so that the items are easy to fetch, and easy to put away again.

Help the children to count more accurately by reminding them to move each thing out of the way as it is counted, or to put things in a line.

Estimating is not just guessing; an estimate should be based on previous experience of counting accurately. For example, if a child has counted out thirty buttons a number of times, then he should be able to look at a pile of buttons and say whether he thinks there are more or less than thirty. So he might estimate: 'I think there are about twenty.' As children's counting improves, they will begin to get better at estimating how many objects are in a group, for a larger range of numbers.

Counting equipment will also be useful when children start to investigate ways of calculating using larger and larger numbers. Some children may need to continue using individual counting equipment (rather than equipment grouped in tens and ones: see pages 18 and 19) for quite a long time, particularly when they are working with totals up to about 40. Recognising how long it takes them to work out answers by counting with equipment in ones will help them, later, to appreciate why people use tens and ones instead.

Ask children and their families to help you collect counting equipment, and look out for appropriate things to buy at jumble sales and in toy shops and department stores.

These ladybirds were bought from a craft shop

Page 54 provides a photocopiable sheet that can be used as a letter for parents and carers.

counting

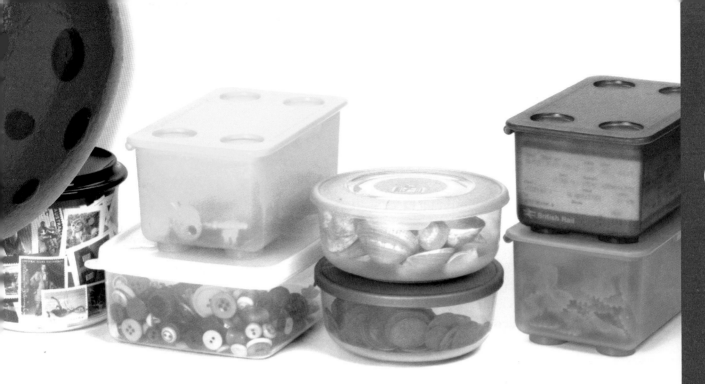

Buy or collect plastic tubs and storage boxes, such as sandwich boxes or ice-cream tubs, to store your collection of counting equipment.

The children can keep a running total of each item collected, or choose a target number. For example: 'Can we get thirty old keys by Friday?'

Use each box of equipment for counting, estimating, to help with calculations, or as tokens in games. Here are some ideas.

Take a handful

Tell the child to take a handful of coins from the box and ask a partner to guess how many she picked up. Both children then count to see how many she really got. They can take turns to do this.

Pick a card

Children choose a card from a set numbered 20 to 50 and count out that many things. A partner is then asked to check.

Fill a dish

Ask a child to fill a small bowl or dish with buttons. How many did you need?

Now try it with something else. Did you need more, or fewer?

Reading and writing numbers to 100

Learning to read and write numbers larger than ten follows a similar pattern to learning the numbers up to ten. Children need plenty of practice in recognising and saying each number before they are expected to write it.

It is important to link counting practice and number recognition by using single items to count (especially for numbers 11 to 20), as well as counting equipment organised in tens and ones.

The 'teen' numbers can be especially confusing for low-attaining children. They need to understand that although we *say* 'fourteen', putting the 'four' at the beginning of the number, we *write* '14'. Numbers from 20 onwards are more logical in how they are said and written, but earlier uncertainty about the order may lead to children reading '31' as 'thirteen', or '42' as 'twenty-four'. Reassure children that most numbers follow a logical pattern: **27 is 20 and 7!**

Children should use all sorts of numbers for a wide variety of activities. Challenge them to find the numbers to match a collection they have counted, or choose a number to count out.

Single numerals can be put together to make larger numbers.

Use magnetic numerals, number counters and tablets, digit cards, door numbers, and any others you can find.

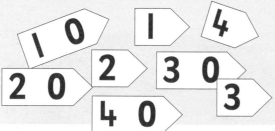

Number cards 0 to 30,

then 0 to 100.

Place value cards (sometimes called arrow cards or corner cards) are invaluable in helping children see, for example, that 'fifty-seven' is written '57' rather than '507'. There is a photocopiable sheet for you to make your own place value cards up to 99 on page 55.

Number spotting

Ask children to look for numbers all around them – on clocks, rulers, doors, cars, calculators, video timers or telephones. Make a display or a book of numbers.

Check children's handwriting

Ensure that children are writing the numerals 0 to 9 correctly.

Suggest that they look out for some of the more common problems, such as:

Is this a 6 or a 0?

1 | Is this a 7 or a 1?

S | Is this a 5 or a back-to-front 2?

For more detailed help, see *Extra Help in Maths: Ages 5–7*, pages 34 and 35, and the photocopiable sheet on page 56 in this book.

Peer coaching

Ask the children to find a partner, and then to look at a page of each other's number work. Can they find a *good* 0, 1, 2, 3, 4, 5, 6, 7, 8 *and* 9 on their friend's page?

Encourage the children to make suggestions about how they could help each other to improve their handwriting. Which numbers do they think their partners have most trouble with? What do they need to do to improve?

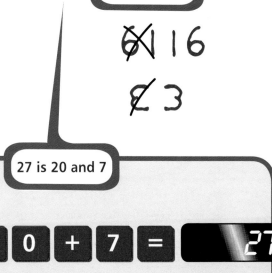

sixteen

Minimise reversals

Children may reverse a single digit, or transpose the digits in a two-digit number.

Encourage the children to check before they write, if they feel unsure about which way round a number goes. Remind them that there are lots of different things they could use to help them – they could look on a number line, a metre rule, a tape measure, a hundred square, or their own 'prompt card'.

Children can also check by thinking about 'how to make that number'. They could use a calculator or place value cards to help.

27 is 20 and 7

$2 \quad 0 \quad + \quad 7 \quad = \quad 27$

20 | 7 → 2|7

Extra Help in Maths
Ages 7–9 NC Level 2 Scottish Level B

Counting in tens and ones

When children start counting collections of more than twenty things, they sometimes make mistakes because they lose concentration or get interrupted!

Show children how to make counting easier by putting things in rows or groups of ten, so that you can count like this:

ten,   twenty,   thirty,   thirty one,   thirty two.

Counting in tens is quicker, more accurate and easier to check than counting a collection one item at a time. It is important, however, that children understand they will get the same total whichever way they count. Encourage them to try counting a collection both singly, and in tens and ones, to compare.

One common mistake that children make, especially when they have only just become confident about counting in tens, is to count like this:

ten,   twenty,   thirly,   forty,   fifty.

Make sure they spot where they should stop counting in tens, and need to change to counting in ones instead. If they have trouble with this, return to counting each item individually for a while.

When children gain confidence with counting up to about 50 using groups of ten and individual items, they will see the sense in making their own tens and ones equipment to help with arithmetic. They will also be able to use purpose-made tens and ones equipment, such as Dienes' and Multibase, more confidently.

I'll count in ones.

One, two, three, four, five...

I'll put things in groups of ten, then count in tens and ones.

Ten, twenty, thirty, forty, forty-one, forty-two.

Counting race

Take turns at counting the same collection of things.

- Time each other in seconds. Which method is quicker?
- Use coffee jar lids to help with counting: put ten things in each.

counting

Make tens and ones equipment

Use everyday items, perhaps those collected for a 'counting library' (see pages 14 and 15), to make tens and ones equipment. Store each set in a sandwich box or similar container. Put about ten 'tens' and twenty 'ones' in each box.

● Thread buttons or beads together in tens.

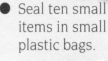

● Keep bundles of ten drinking straws together with elastic bands.

● Use pieces of pipe-cleaner to tie ten old keys in a bunch.

● Seal ten small items in small plastic bags.

Use place value cards and counting equipment

I can find the right cards to match the number I've counted...

5 3

7 0   6   7 6

...or choose a tens card and a ones card, then count out that many.

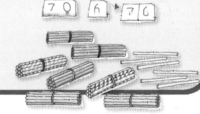

Practise counting in tens and more than ten ones

Practise counting collections where only some of the items have been put into tens:

ten,   twenty,   thirty,   thirty-one,   thirty-two,   thirty-three,   thirty-four,   thirty-five,

thirty-six,   thirty-seven,   thirty-eight,   thirty-nine,   forty,   forty-one,   forty-two

Count backwards, too. Take away keys one at a time, until you get down to thirty. Then count down in tens.

Board games

Board games can provide very useful practice at counting increasingly large numbers, including counting in ones, in tens and ones, and in twos, fives or tens.

Children who have used and adapted track games will be more confident about using board games.

Board games work best when played by two or three people working together. With more than three players, individual children will spend too much time waiting for a turn. Children can also work on their own, using two counters to represent two different players – for example: 'See whether the fish or the spider gets to the end first.'

Board games are easy to make and easy to adapt, and they provide sufficient variety to keep children's interest and concentration. Children can make their own games to use in school or at home, although they may need to be given dice and counters to keep at home.

Making boards

Start with a board drawn on a large sheet of paper, with three or four rows of ten spaces. Help the children to write the numbers in the spaces, as shown here.

21	22	23							
18	17	16	15	14	13	12	11
2	3	4	5	6	7	8	9	10

Children who sometimes reverse digits may find it very difficult to fill in numbers on this row, if they have to work from right to left.

Help by counting along from 11 to 20; write 20 and 19 for them; then let them fill in 18, 17, 16, …, 11.

Dice and counters

When you have made your board, choose a dice and some counters to play with.

Use small toys, coloured bricks, or child-made tokens as counters.

Change the dice to change the speed of the game. Throw one dice, or throw two and add the scores.

Change counters to change the context of the game.

Make boards in rows of 5 or 10 spaces, going up to 30, 50 or 100.

30	29	28	27	26
21	Go on 5	23	24	25
20	19	18	Go back 4	16
11	12	13	14	15
10	Go on 3	8	7	6
1	2	3	4	5

Add special spaces: Go back 4   Go on 10

'Loop' board games are
very adaptable.

win 3

win 4

win 5

First to 25

First to 25

This game practises counting
to 25. Each child puts a
counter on a blank space to
start, then throws a dice and
moves that many spaces.

Choose any box of counting
equipment to play with. If a counter
lands on a 'win' space, the player takes
that many items.

Keep going until you have collected 25 items.

You need a dice, a
counter each, and lots of
objects to collect.

win 6

win 7

win 2

**Draw your own
track, or use the
photocopiable
sheet on page 57.**

Practise counting

For variety, change the counting equipment, or draw a new track with different 'win' spaces,
or a different target total.

First to 30 — win 2, win 4, win 2, win 2, win 4

First to 50 — win 5, win 10, win 5, win 5, win 10, win 5

First to 100 — win 30, win 10, win 20, win 20, win 10, win 20

Practise counting in twos,   in fives   and in tens.

Making one hundred

Being able to count to 100 is an important milestone for children. When they first start counting, one hundred seems like an enormous number but, as children gain in confidence and can consistently and accurately count groups of thirty, forty or fifty objects, 100 begins to seem quite manageable!

Provide children with time to count and make groups of 100 in a variety of ways, to help them get a 'feel' for the size of this important number. As well as looking at 100 things in a long line (in the same pattern as a number line), find opportunities to make ten rows of ten (in the same pattern as a hundred square). Count forward to 100 in tens, and then remove ten at a time and count back down to nought.

Arrays

- Make an array of ten rows of ten sequins or stickers.

  You don't have to do this all in one session. Glue on 20 sequins every day for a week!

- Try other arrays, such as five rows of 20, four rows of 25, or two rows of 50.

- Put one hundred pennies in rows or piles of ten, or in one long line.

- Take turns with a partner to fill a ten by ten pegboard with pegs. Fill each row with a different colour to the row before.

Rubber stamps

Print one hundred pictures in a row, and number them 1 to 100.

Thread beads

Thread one hundred beads on a string.

21	22	23	24	25	26	27	28	29	30
31	32	33	34	35	36	37	38	39	40
41	42	43	44	45	46	47	48	49	50
51	52	53	54	55	56	57	58	59	60
61	62	63	64	65	66	67	68	69	70
71	72	73	74	75	76	77	78	79	80
81	82	83	84	85	86	87	88		
91	92	93	94	95	96	97			100

Hundred square

Put a counter on every number on a hundred square. (There is a photocopiable hundred square on page 58.)

Number cards

Spread out a pack of 1 to 100 number cards in rows of ten.

Collections

Make collections of exactly one hundred things.

Packs of 100

Find examples of things that are sold in hundreds...
...and count them!

Numbers in order

Practice at counting out loud, both forwards and backwards, helps children to become confident about using numbers to 100. Children need to listen to other people counting in ones, in twos and in tens, and to count out loud (and in their heads) themselves, sometimes using number lines and hundred squares for support.

Counting backwards is much more difficult than counting forwards, especially when 'crossing the tens'. For example, children may be unsure of what number comes next after: '44, 43, 42, 41, 40…'.

Some children are so comfortable with the rhythm of counting forwards that they will change direction when they are counting backwards, without realising they have done so: '43, 42, 41, 40, 41, 42, 43, 44…'. Watch out, too, for children who start to reverse the digits of the numbers they are reading when they use a number line from right to left, to count down – for example, reading '34' as 'forty-three'.

Putting small groups of numbers in order of size, and deciding which is the biggest or smallest number in a group, are activities that can help children develop a real 'feel' for where numbers fit on the number line. The number line provides a powerful mental image for many people when they are thinking about addition and subtraction, or about rounding numbers. (See pages 36 and 37.) It can also help children see number patterns – for example: 'If we highlight every other number, starting with one, we generate the numbers we call odd numbers.'

Watch and say

Together, watch a digital timer count seconds up to 59, or click on a tally counter up to 100, and say the numbers as they appear.

Use a calculator to count down from 100. Different calculators work in different ways. Try this:

1 0 0 – 1 = = =

and keep pressing the equals sign. Or this:

1 0 0 – 1 = – 1 =

and so on.

Make a tape

Make a simple counting tape for children to use with a partner. Record yourself on a cassette, counting from zero to 100, 100 to zero, counting in tens to 100, and back to zero. Later, add counting in twos to 100 and back.

fifty-one, fifty…

Children take turns to play the tape to their partner, who joins in with counting out loud. One player can press the pause button on the tape machine at any point and ask the partner to say what the next number will be.

…forty-nine

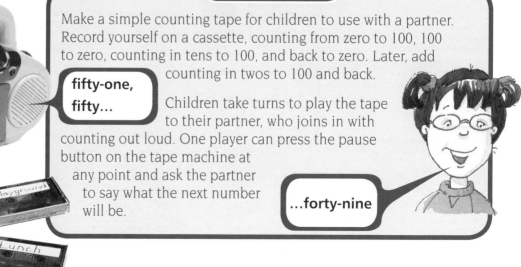

counting

Dot-to-dot pictures

Use dot-to-dot pictures in books from newsagents or supermarkets.

Join the dots from 0 to 50. Or work backwards, and do dot-to-dot pictures starting from the biggest number.

ILLUS © 2001, JO MOORE FROM HOW TO HANDLE YOUR CAT BY ROY APPS © 2001, ROY APPS (HIPPO)

Take 3 cards

Work with a partner. Shuffle a pack of 0 to 50 number cards (or cards up to 100). One player takes three cards and gives them to his or her partner, who must then put them in order, smallest first, as quickly as possible. Take turns to do this and check on a number line.

Try this, too: take three cards and pick the largest or the smallest of the set.

Find the page

Find non-fiction books with up to 96 pages. Look at the page numbers, and talk about how to use Contents pages and Index pages.

Which page are you up to in your reading book?

Ask children to number the pages in their exercise books.

Peg up odds and evens

You need a 'washing line' made of string, some pegs and number cards from 0 to 20. Peg the numbers, in order, on the line, facing forwards.

Then turn alternate cards around, so only their backs can be seen. Ask the child to read the sequence that he or she can see. Then go round to the other side of the line, and read that sequence.

Try this with cards numbered 20 to 40, or 40 to 60…

Say and count odds and evens

Use cards numbered 1 to 30 and a box of counting equipment. Pick a card for a partner. She or he must count out that many things, and put them in pairs. Is there an odd one left over? Is that number odd or even? Take turns at this.

Extra Help in Maths
Ages 7–9 NC Level 2 Scottish Level B

Extra help
with **calculations**

This book concentrates on building the skills and understanding of children who have made a start on simple practical and mental arithmetic with numbers under ten. For more detailed information about earlier work, please see *Extra Help in Maths: Ages 5–7, NC Level 1*.

Practical approach

Addition and subtraction should always be introduced to children in contexts that make sense to them, using numbers that they can count confidently and accurately. Increase children's confidence by providing practical equipment and representational materials to help them understand and solve problems. For example, provide toy cars for a problem like this: '*There were 4 cars in the car park. Then 5 more drove in. How many cars altogether?*' Working with more abstract materials such as counters or cubes is also helpful. Children can use them to represent the items in their sums. Encourage them to use their fingers to represent objects too!

Many children find that drawing a problem helps them understand what to do, especially in the early stages of learning about addition and subtraction, or multiplication and division. Children's drawings of problems will often simplify as they realise they do not need detailed pictures to reach a conclusion.

Develop mental skills

Gradually, children become able to imagine objects in their heads, rather than always needing to see or handle them to carry out a calculation. This is an important step in developing mental calculation skills.

The number line is an important tool for practising counting, addition and subtraction, and imagining a number line in your head can also help develop mental skills. The 'empty' number line, where only the numbers needed in a calculation are marked, is an especially powerful model to use. However, the idea of a number line is quite abstract, and low-attaining children may need extra time and practice to appreciate how to use one.

Jamie's drawings of 4 cars, then 5 cars, became less detailed as he worked on this problem.

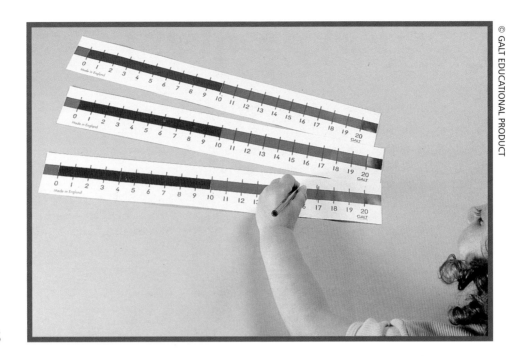

Making links

Children who have already worked on addition and subtraction with numbers up to 10 will have started to use the symbols +, – and =. Using a calculator can help to consolidate their successful use of these symbols, and can aid with the introduction of early work on multiplication. The links between addition and subtraction, and those between addition and multiplication, can also be explored using practical and mental methods. For example, show the links between 8, 5 and 3 with practical equipment:

$$3 + 5 = 8 \qquad 5 + 3 = 8$$
$$8 - 5 = 3 \qquad 8 - 3 = 5$$

Use a calculator to show that $4 + 4 + 4 + 4 + 4$ (5 lots of 4) gives the same answer as 5×4, and

© BANANASTOCK LTD

demonstrate this with practical equipment too. Early informal work on division is also appropriate at this stage, especially sharing between two.

Counting practice

Counting practice continues to be important as children's skills in addition and subtraction grow. When they start to work within totals larger than 20, counting equipment that includes 'groups' of ten becomes useful. Help children to make their own 'tens' equipment, so that they understand that they can use a ten, a ten and four ones to make 24, or they can count out 24 individual items.

Varied contexts

When children become familiar with carrying out particular sums, they will begin to use more efficient strategies to carry out calculations, both practically and mentally. They will also begin to know some number facts by heart. At this stage, they will need to be given problems set in varied contexts so that they can practise using their skills. Shopping and money is a particularly helpful context to use.

See pages 28 to 45 for further information and activities.

Practical problems

As soon as children are able to count consistently and accurately within a particular range of numbers, they can start work on calculations within that range. Addition and subtraction should always be introduced with an emphasis on practical, oral and mental work, using understandable contexts.

Children may not always record their work on paper at first and, when they do, it may be by drawing pictures and giving a single number as the answer, rather than writing a complete sum. Problems set in a context that is easy to describe orally can take a child a very long time to write down. Children need to be shown that using numbers, and the symbols +, – and =, offers a very economical way of explaining what we did.

Children's methods for adding and taking away will become more sophisticated as they gain experience. It is important to give them opportunities to explore and explain methods of their own, and to listen to others explaining how they have worked something out. Children need to realise that one of the skills of a good mathematician is being able to choose a method to suit a particular calculation.

Once they have used equipment representing a variety of contexts, children will increasingly be able to 'picture' problems in their heads, and will not always need to use equipment. With some sums, children will have worked out the answers so often that they know them by heart.

People on the bus

Use the bus counting cards made from photocopiable page 52 for this activity.

Children can take two cards from a set of 0 to 10 (or 0 to 15) number cards to get the numbers for their sum, or just choose their own numbers.

Many activities suitable for counting practice can be used for addition and subtraction too. The games on pages 12 and 13, for example, provide contexts for straightforward problems.

'People' to go on the buses

We're counting people.

It's my turn to make up a problem. There are 8 people upstairs on the bus, and 4 people downstairs. How many altogether?

We each have a bus card.

Making totals

- Children can use a game to investigate all the ways to make a particular total with two numbers.

- They can draw or write about their findings

$11 + 2 = 13$

$3 + 10 = 13$

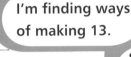
I'm finding ways of making 13.

8 snakes in the lake, and 5 on the bank.

$$0 + 13 = 13$$
$$7 + 6 = 13$$
$$11 + 2 = 13$$
$$8 + 5 = 13$$
$$9 + 4 = 13$$
$$10 + 3 = 13$$

Using a calculator

Using a calculator with counting equipment is a good way of emphasising the symbols +, − and =. Ask the children to work in pairs and take turns to make up problems.

There were 11 spiders on a web. Then 4 ran away. How many were left?

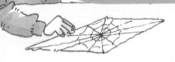

Eleven take away four equals…

- Both children try to work out the sum in their heads.

- Then one child uses a web and 'spiders' (see page 13) while her partner uses a calculator.

- When they have agreed on the correct answer, they write the sum down.

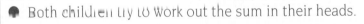
$$11 - 4 = 7 ✔$$

For the next sum, they swap, and the first child has the calculator.

Remember that when children take responsibility for making up their own sums, they will often be more ambitious than you would expect. They may also have ideas for making or collecting other practical equipment.

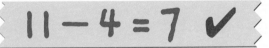
I had 14 pencils.
I gave half of them to my friend.
How many did I have left?

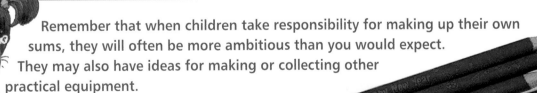

© SODA

Adding with tens and ones

When children begin to tackle additions with totals larger than 20, counting equipment that includes 'groups' of ten, like that shown on page 19, becomes useful.

For example, if you want to calculate 14 + 24 using equipment, it is quicker (and usually more accurate) to count a ten and four ones, then add two tens and four ones, than to use 'fourteen add twenty-four' individual items. At first, though, some children will feel more confident using just ones or, alternatively, using tens and ones but still counting each item in the tens separately.

Children who use 'home-made' tens and ones equipment alongside individual items of counting equipment will soon see the advantages of having 'ready-made' groups of ten. They are also more likely to be confident about using wooden or plastic tens and ones equipment. Explain that such equipment is made especially to help children do sums.

One important aspect of using counting equipment to carry out calculations is that it can help children see that no matter what order you add in, you should still get the same answer. It will also help them to see that adding nothing (zero or nought) will leave the total the same.

Another advantage is that children can show you how they have calculated a sum by moving equipment to demonstrate. Increased familiarity with using equipment can help children build mental pictures of a calculation until they no longer need to use the tens and ones at all.

Choose a card

Use a pack of cards numbered 10 to 50, and some tens and ones equipment. Ask the children to work with a partner.

Choose a card… make that number… then add two.

Twenty-six add two equals twenty-eight.

Explain that they should repeat the activity until they are sure they can always work it out in their heads. Then try these:

Choose a card… add twenty.

Choose a card… add three.

Choose a card… add thirty.

Choose a card… add four.

Choose a card… add forty.

Ask the children to write down some of their sums, then to make up 'choose a card… add' rules of their own. Change the range of cards they use; for example, use 30 to 70.

Tens and ones and the hundred square

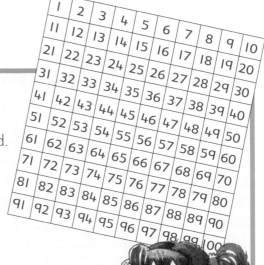

Use tens and ones equipment alongside a hundred square to investigate what happens when ten is added.

For example, try 46 + 10 on the hundred square, by counting along ten spaces:

| 41 | 42 | 43 | 44 | 45 | ⑭46 | 47 | 48 | 49 | 50 |
| 51 | 52 | 53 | 54 | 55 | 56 | 57 | 58 | 59 | 60 |

Then do 46 + 10 with tens and ones:

Fifty-six.

Try this with lots of different starting numbers. Try adding 20, or 30.

Place value cards and tens and ones

1 0	1
2 0	2
3 0	3
4 0	4

Use these numbers from a set of place value cards, and some tens and ones equipment.

Choose a 'tens' and a 'ones' card to make a number, then make another number.

Add the two numbers together.

3 2   4 1

Write down the sum like this: 32 + 41 = 73

Do as many of these as you can.

Then play some more, adding in these extra 'ones' cards to choose from:

5   6   7   8   9

3 6

1 5

I did 30 + 10 + 6 + 5 = 51.

Extra Help in Maths
Ages 7–9 NC Level 2 Scottish Level B

31

Subtraction

Most children find subtraction significantly more difficult than addition, and it is sensible to spend time reviewing work with numbers below 20 before moving on to larger numbers. Children need to spend time looking at subtraction in three different ways: taking away; finding the difference; and complementary addition. Make sure each of them is set in a sensible context.

Firstly, look at 'taking away'. Use counting equipment like that shown on pages 12 and 13, and make up problems like: *'There were 15 people on the bus, then 9 people got off. How many people were left on the bus?'* Children can count out the starting number of people, take away the number who got off, and see how many are left. Using a calculator alongside counting equipment helps emphasise the minus sign, as the child checks.

$$1\ 5\ -\ 9\ =\ 6$$

'Finding the difference' between two numbers occurs in problems like: *'This football costs £15 and that one is £9. What is the difference in their prices?'* Children can place 15 counters as pretend pound coins in a row, then nine 'coins' alongside them, to see that there is a difference of six.

Sometimes, a subtraction problem is most easily solved by 'complementary addition'. For example: *'I want to buy a football that costs £15. I've got £9. How much more do I need?'* The most natural way for children to solve this is to count on from 9 to 15, to see that they need another £6. In other words, children can turn the problem into a 'missing number' problem:

$$9 + \boxed{} = 15$$

Working in context is important so that children see why you can add numbers in any order, but you *can't* subtract in any order. If you change the order, you change the story too much! For example, *'There were 9 people on the bus, then 15 people got off,'* is just not possible.

Start with 20

Ask the children to work with a partner, using a ten and ten 'ones', or twenty individual items, and a 0 to 9 dice.

Start with 20; throw the dice; take away that number.

$$20 - 2 = 18$$

Write down your calculation each time.

Try 'Start with 30' or 'Start with 40'.

Can you do them in your head?

Tens and ones and the hundred square

Investigate what happens when you take away ten. (See page 31 for adding.)

For example, try 88 – 10 on the hundred square, by counting back ten squares.

Then try 88 – 10 using tens and ones.

Seventy-eight.

Try this with lots of different starting numbers.
Try taking away 20, or 30.

Horse race

Use a big sheet of paper, two plastic horses, and a dice.

Draw a race track, making sure that each space is big enough for two horses. Number the spaces.

Throw a 0 to 9 dice to decide how many spaces each horse can move, each turn.

Keep asking, 'Which horse is winning? How many spaces is it ahead?'

Count on the track, and check with a calculator.

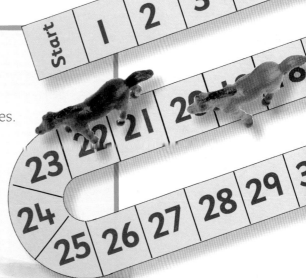

$$2\ 2\ -\ 1\ 9\ =\ 3$$

Take away one

Use ten little bags of ten items.

One child gives his partner some of the bags and asks her to count how many items there are, and to tell him the number that is one less than that.

I've got 50.
One less than
50 is 49.

Learning number facts

As children become confident with counting and estimating numbers up to 20, and particularly as they gain experience of addition and subtraction within a total of ten, they begin to realise that there are more and more sums that they do not need to calculate, because they already know the answers by heart.

Each child's repertoire of 'quick-recall' facts needs to be increased gradually, and the sums they memorise must always be ones that they have already calculated many times, so they understand how the answers are reached. Knowing a good range of number facts helps children to be more successful at mental, practical and, later on, pencil and paper arithmetic.

Short but frequent practice sessions are the most effective. Working with a partner, or alone, is the way most children build fluency quickly. Participation in group and whole-class practice is helpful too, but may not include sufficient repetition of target facts to be enough on its own. Practice at home is *definitely* useful, so look for ways of involving family or friends outside school time.

© SCOTT CAMPBELL/SODA

Keep the number of facts that you expect children to learn at any one time quite low, and recognise that some children's ability to memorise successfully may be limited. Instead, concentrate on helping individual children to find strategies for working things out quickly. Make sure that you provide enjoyable opportunities for children to practise and use their existing knowledge of number facts frequently, to maintain their speed and confidence.

Number families

A number 'family' is the term sometimes given to the group of addition and subtraction facts related to a particular number. For example, the facts for 3 are:

$0 + 3 = 3$	$1 + 2 = 3$	$2 + 1 = 3$	$3 + 0 = 3$
$3 - 0 = 3$	$3 - 1 = 2$	$3 - 2 = 1$	$3 - 3 = 0$

Investigating groups of linked sums like this helps children to begin to see patterns in number relationships, and thus helps them to learn the facts more quickly. Ask them to try these:

- Write a '4 or 5?' test for a partner, where all the answers will be 4 or 5.

- Make a poster for the 'family' of 6. Take it home to help with learning those facts.

$2 + 2 =$
$3 + 2 =$
$0 + 5 =$

- Write each fact for 7 on a piece of card. There will be 16 cards altogether.

$0+7$	$1+6$	$2+5$	$3+4$	$4+3$	$5+2$	$6+1$	$7+0$
$7-0$	$7-1$	$7-2$	$7-3$	$7-4$	$7-5$	$7-6$	$7-7$

The children shuffle the cards and test themselves!

- Think of ways to practise the facts for 8 and 9. Choose one of the methods used for 4, 5, 6 or 7.

Two cards for ten

Give a pair of children the number cards from a pack of playing cards, so they have the numbers 1 to 10 four times. They should shuffle the cards, then, working together, see how quickly they can put them out in pairs that make 10. Highlight 10 + 0 by asking: *What card would there need to be to go with 10?*

Doubles on display

Use a photo frame to display a 'doubles' fact to learn. Keep it on your desk until everyone knows it. Then write a new doubles fact to take its place.

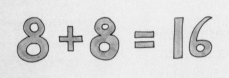

$$8 + 8 = 16$$

Spin some, say some

Draw a card like this and stand a spinner on it.

Working with a partner, children take turns to spin the spinner, and ask: *'How much more would you need to make ten?'*

Tens, too!

Use all the 'tens' cards from a set of place value cards. Put them face down on the table. Turn a card over. Ask: *'How much more would you need to make one hundred?'*

Dice practice

Use two 0 to 5 dice, or 1 to 6 dice, or 0 to 9 dice. Throw the dice and ask the child to say the total as quickly as possible.

Eight add nine is seventeen.

addition and subtraction

Using the number line

The 'number line' is a very powerful mathematical tool that many children find helpful when they are counting, adding or taking away. The ability to picture a number line in your head can help to develop mental skills.

© BANANASTOCK LTD

Initial activities on a number line should concentrate on encouraging children to see numbers in order, and making them familiar with 'hopping' forwards and backwards, one step at a time. Children can then start to use the line for addition, using increasingly efficient strategies, and for subtraction. The abstract nature of arithmetic on number lines lends itself to practising a wider range of vocabulary for addition and subtraction.

Number lines can be a useful way of pointing out number patterns, such as the multiples of two, five or ten. They can also be useful when introducing children to the idea of rounding numbers to the nearest ten.

The idea of an 'empty' number line, where only the numbers needed for the specific calculation are marked, can help children to carry out calculations and explain how they did them. When doing calculations in your head, it can be helpful to write down interim numbers, and an empty number line provides a simple structure for doing that.

> Draw your own number line, as long as you need, or use ready-made number lines.

Check that children have used a number line before. If not, some of the activities in *Extra Help in Maths: Ages 5–7 (NC Level 1/Scottish Level A)* may prove useful.

Missing numbers

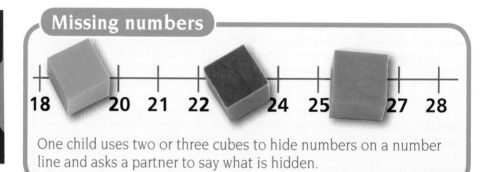

18   20 21 22   24 25   27 28

One child uses two or three cubes to hide numbers on a number line and asks a partner to say what is hidden.

Adding up

3 2

6

Make a two-digit number and a single-digit number from place value cards. Add them together on the number line:

Start here.

30 31 32 33 34 35 36 37 38 39 40

32 + 6 = 38

Start with the bigger number...

...because it saves work!

Sometimes children's answers are one out, because they have started counting on the initial number. In the example above, they might count '32, 33, 34, 35, 36, 37'. Emphasise adding the first one: *'We've got 32 add 6. 32 add 1 gets us to 33, then we keep on adding… 2, 3, 4, 5, 6. We're at 38!'*

Taking away

Make a two-digit number from place value cards. Throw a dice to see how much to take away.

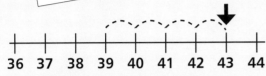

Make an arrow from card, to show where you started.

| | | | | | | | | |
|36|37|38|39|40|41|42|43|44|

$$43 - 4 = 39$$

Ten more, ten less

One child chooses a number on the number line, and asks a partner a 'ten more' or 'ten less' question, such as: 'What's *ten more than* 13?'

13 14 15 16 17 18 19 20 21 22 23

They take turns at this, until they feel confident.

Ten strip

18 19 20 21 22 23 24 25 26 27 28

A 'ten strip' can make it easier to add or subtract ten. Just cut a piece of card exactly the length of ten spaces on your number line.

$$18 + 10 = 28$$

Empty number lines

Introduce the idea of drawing your own number line to help you as you do a sum in your head:

What's 5 + 8? **Start with 8.** **Add 2 to get to 10.** **That leaves 3 more.** **It's 13!**

0   8   +2   10   +3   13

Discuss different ways of doing the same sum in your head, using the empty number line to show what you did:

What's 15 + 35?

0   35   +5   40   +10   50   0   35   +10   45   +5   50

Early multiplication and division

Multiplication is a speedier alternative to adding, when we need to find a total of lots of groups of the same number, or to work out how many things are in an array (several equal rows of objects).

Early work on number patterns helps to make children familiar with the multiples they will eventually begin to learn by heart. For example, it is useful to practise counting in fives along the number line from 0 to 50, or in tens from 0 to 100 and back again, as these are the answers to the 5 and 10 times tables. At this level, children should become familiar wi-the multiples of 2, 5 and 10.

Doubling numbers is, of course, the same as multiplying them by two. Practise both doubling: *'What's double 7?'* and working backwards: *'I doubled a number and I got 14. What was my number?'* **t**o link doubling and halving. Checking with a calculator helps to demonstrate the method used to write down a doubling statement using the multiplication sign: $2 \times 7 = 14$ (or $7 \times 2 = 14$). The calculator is particularly useful in drawing children's attention to the difference between the + and × signs.

Multiplication is an alternative to repeated addition. For example, instead of $5 + 5 + 5 + 5 + 5 + 5$, we can say, *'Six lots of five,'* and write the problem as 6×5 (or 5×6). Children who do not yet know this tables fact by heart will still use repeated addition to get an answer (unless they use a calculator or a tables chart), but will begin to see that writing a multiplication is quicker and clearer than the equivalent addition. At this stage, the most important focus is on understanding what to do and being able to work out an answer accurately. Learning tables facts by heart and increasing each child's fluency with rapid recall will follow.

Draw a number line

Show a counting sequence by drawing a number line. This line shows multiples of five.

```
+--+--+--+--+--+--+--+--+--+--+--+--+--+--+--+
0  1  2  3  4  5  6  7  8  9  10 11 12 13 14 15
```

A number line like this helps children to see that the 'fives' are in a regular pattern.

Halving and doubling

Two children shuffle cards numbered 0 to 10. One child takes a card, and asks his partner to double that number. Then they check on a calculator.

They can take turns at this. Use cards 11 to 15, too.

Alternatively, the first child takes a card *without* telling the partner the number, and doubles it. The partner then has to work out what the original number was.

Double my number is 16. What's my card?

Flip-ups

Make these to practise counting in twos or fives. There are some photocopiable flip-ups on page 59 to get you started.

- Cut an A4 piece of paper in half lengthwise. Use one piece to make a flip-up.

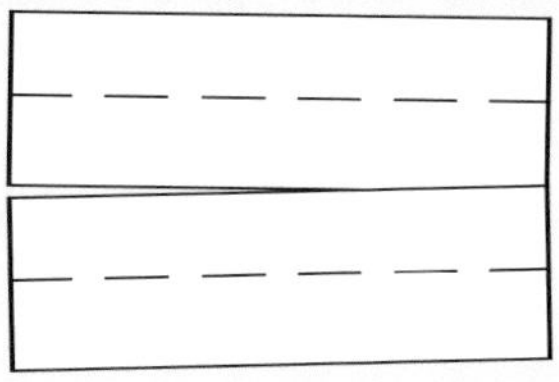

- Fold the paper in half, then open it out again.

- Draw lines across, to split it into six or seven spaces.

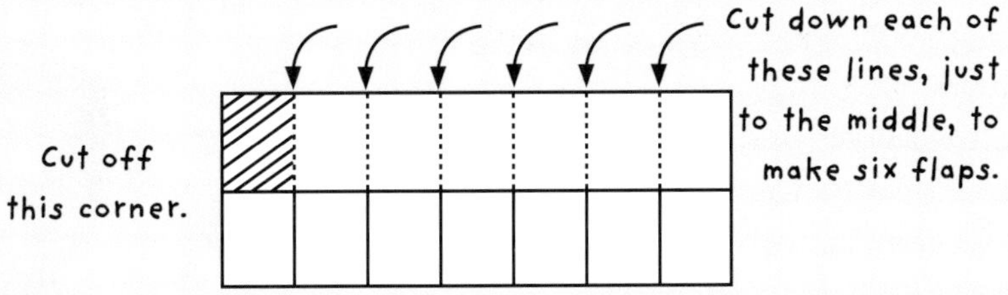

Cut off this corner.

Cut down each of these lines, just to the middle, to make six flaps.

- Draw or print five smiley faces in each of the six spaces under the flaps. Write 'How many faces?' in the first space.

- Take turns with a partner. Decide how many flaps to flip up, and ask 'How many faces?'

- Make a longer flip-up by sticking two pieces of paper together.

How many faces?

- Draw or print two things in each space, to practise multiples of two, or print five things in each space to practise multiples of five.

1 2 3 4 **5**

6 7 8 9 **10**

Five stamps and change direction!

Stamp about in a hall or playground to practise multiples of fives. Count out loud; stamp or make a 'star' with your arms stretched high when you get to each multiple of five; then set off in a different direction. Try counting backwards, too, from 50 to zero.

Extra Help in **Maths**
Ages 7–9 NC Level 2 Scottish Level B

39

Money

Money provides a very useful everyday context for realistic problems in addition and subtraction, as well as multiplication and division.

It is especially helpful for two particular aspects of subtraction: giving change by the 'shopkeeper's method' of counting up, and finding differences, for example between two prices.

Begin by checking children's ability to recognise coins of different denominations. Use real coins to do this. Children do not have to be able to recognise all eight coins before they start 'shopping' activities; just limit the coins used to the ones with which the children are familiar, or those you wish them to concentrate on learning. Make £5 and £10 notes, too, and use them for counting up to £100. By making their own notes, children will also be gaining purposeful practice in writing £ signs.

When you count up how much money you have in a handful of small change, you are, in effect, adding several small numbers together. Reading a price and finding the right coins is a similar problem. Adding two or more prices (using either just pence, or just pounds, but not a mixture at this level) is another way of practising adding.

Reading £ signs

Ask the children to look at adverts in a newspaper to see how many different £ signs they can find. Cut them out and stick them on a sheet of paper to emphasise the variety of ways the £ sign can be printed.

Writing £ signs

Ask the child to write a £ sign for you.

If you feel he or she needs further practice, try this method:

- Using a broad felt-tipped pen, write five or six of these, quite large, while the child watches you.

Always start at the top

- Give the child the pen to have a go.

- Go back and put the lines on yours, then give the child the pen to complete the ones he or she has drawn.

- Repeat this exercise every now and then, reducing the thickness of the pen and the size of the £ signs each time you practise.

Make £10 notes

Show the children a real £10 note, if possible, then ask them to make some of their own on buff-coloured paper. Keep checking how much money you have made, as you go along.

Tens and ones

- Use £10 notes and 'pound coins' (either plastic coins, buttons or counters), or use 10p and 1p coins (real ones if possible) to practise counting in tens and ones.

- Give some money to your partner. How quickly can she or he say how much there is?

- Ask your partner for some money. Check you have been given the right amount.

- Make up sums for each other. Write some of them down. Use money to help you calculate the answers.

> **What's £26 add £15?**

> **I spent 18p then 24p. How much altogether?**

> **I had £50. I spent £35. How much did I have left?**

Mega money

Use 'mega money' (large scale replica card coins) or ordinary 5p coins to practise counting in fives. Start with ten 5p coins. Give some to your partner. How quickly can he or she tell you how much money they have?

Role play and money

Role play can provide excellent opportunities for talking, drawing and writing about mathematical problem-solving in the world around us.

Wherever possible, visit shops and stores like those you are going to set up for role play, to give you and the children ideas of things you could make, collect or do.

Role play using money gives children the time to work at a slower pace than is usually possible in the real world, and enables them to repeat activities until they understand them properly. They can take turns at being customers and shop staff, and find out more about using coins and notes, adding up amounts of money, and giving change.

Use just pence or just pounds for your prices, so that children at this level are working with manageable numbers. Shops with prices in pounds are especially useful as the numbers can stay low but the prices still look realistic, not silly or babyish.

Use real coins if you can. Make £10 notes (see page 41) and collect buttons or counters to be £1 coins. Make price labels, advertising posters and bills. For help with writing pound signs, see page 40.

© THE ROYAL MINT

Baker's shop

Muffins 10p each

Cookies 5p each

Cheese straws 2p each

Sponge drops 1p each

Use play dough or modelling clay to create bread and cakes for a baker's shop. Sell every item for 1p, 2p, 5p or 10p. Take turns to be the shopkeeper and the customer.

4 cookies, please!

They're 5p each. That's 20p, please.

© INGRAM PUBLISHING; PHOTODISC, INC

Bookshops

Collect some books and price them at £1, £2, £5 or £10. Take turns to be the shopkeeper and customer.

Visit a bookshop to look at new books. Talk about why so many books are priced £4.99 instead of £5.

£10

£1 each
or
£5 the set

Antique shop

> If no one wants to buy this, we can put the price down.

This can be a lot of fun to prepare. Similar props could also be used to create a car boot sale, or a 'white elephant' stall at a jumble sale.

Talk about how you decide what price each thing for sale should be.

Prices to the nearest 10p

Set up a 'shop' where everything has prices between 10p and 90p.

19p

> I'm fed up with pennies!

> Let's change the prices, so that customers can always pay using just 10p pieces.

11p each

Use a number line with all the multiples of ten highlighted, to help with rounding to the nearest ten.

0 1 2 3 4 5 6 7 8 9 **10** 11 12 13 14 15 16 17 18 19 **20** 21 22 23 24

Discuss what to do with prices like 25p, 35p and 45p. When will you round up, and when will you round down? It's up to you.

Sums in words

Children need to develop their understanding of solving problems so that they can decide for themselves what information is relevant in a problem, and whether they need to add, subtract, multiply or divide.

It is tempting to make life easier by always giving low-attaining children arithmetic where the decisions have been made for them, and the context (and the words describing it) have been stripped away. This may seem to be a sensible thing to do, especially as children who find mathematics difficult can sometimes find reading difficult too. But it only makes life easier in the short term; it is better to take a longer-term view, and help children tackle maths embedded in real-life problems.

Firstly, look for ways of presenting word problems that do not rely on reading ability. Many of the activities already described in this book use work with practical, imaginative equipment, where children can work in pairs and make up problems for each other, working orally rather than in writing. Sometimes a partner who is a more confident reader can help by reading a problem out loud – or an adult can read and discuss the problem. Sometimes it may be appropriate to put problems on tape, so the child can listen to it repeatedly and work out what to do.

Secondly, look for ways of building reading skills through work on maths problems. Problems set in context can be written like very short stories, and successive problems can use similar vocabulary, providing useful repetition of less-familiar words. Provide a scribe sometimes, to write down problems that children have made up for each other. Find ways of illustrating written problems, perhaps using children's own drawings, to make the context more accessible.

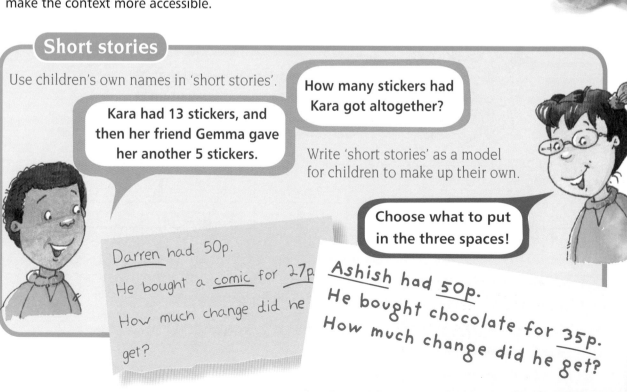

Short stories

Use children's own names in 'short stories'.

Kara had 13 stickers, and then her friend Gemma gave her another 5 stickers.

How many stickers had Kara got altogether?

Write 'short stories' as a model for children to make up their own.

Choose what to put in the three spaces!

Darren had 50p.
He bought a comic for 27p.
How much change did he get?

Ashish had 50p.
He bought chocolate for 35p.
How much change did he get?

Using practical equipment

Give 5 bones each to ☐ dogs.
How many bones altogether?

Give 2 bones each to ☐ dogs.
How many bones altogether?

Give 10 bones each to ☐ dogs.
How many bones altogether?

Match 'stories' to practical equipment, and use a dice or a set of number cards to change each story.

Make 'bones' from pieces of pipe-cleaner.

How many?

Check that you introduce stories that could be solved by addition, subtraction, multiplication and division. Let children choose their own numbers for the spaces in problems like these:

This does not have to be a multiple of 5. In real life, we often have money left over!

Andrew had 10 badges.
He gave ☐ to his friend.
How many did Andrew have left?

Cookies cost 5p each.
I've got ☐ p.
How many cookies can I buy?

Number in words

Practise reading and writing numbers in words, too.

two   three   seven

I bought four cookies.
They were 5p each.
How much did they cost?

Extra Help in **Maths**
Ages 7–9 NC Level 2 Scottish Level B

45

Extra help

with **measures, shape** and **space**

Many topics in measures, shape and space are accessible to children across a wide range of attainment, so it may be easier to work with a whole class than in number work. You may also find that some children who struggle in number have a good 'feel' for shape and space, or vice versa: mathematics is a very varied subject, and people's attainment in different areas of maths can vary, too.

Maths is also a subject that has many links between its different areas, and this can mean that children's low attainment in number work causes them difficulties in measures or shape and space. A child who is not yet confident with recognising the numbers 10 to 30 may be slow to start reading measurements on a ruler, but this does not mean that you have to wait until the child knows all the numbers before beginning to measure. Often children (and adults) learn faster when they can see a useful context and purpose to their learning. However, it is helpful to be aware of potential difficulties and, in the example above, the child's confidence will be boosted if she starts by measuring lengths under 15cm, and then proceeds to lengths of 15cm, 20cm, 25cm and 30cm.

Measures

Which ball is the smallest? Who has the biggest glass of squash? Who can jump the furthest? How long until tea time? Children are interested in measuring and comparing all sorts of things in their everyday lives, and gradually develop an increasingly sophisticated vocabulary to explain what they mean. As with other new words, children need to hear them being used in context, and to say and use them themselves. Bear in mind, though, that the words used to describe the size or quantity of things are all used comparatively. For example, even a word as simple as 'big' depends on the context for its meaning. Think of a big house, a big planet, a big

butterfly – the 'big' is compared to other things of the same sort, so a big butterfly is actually very small compared to a house! This can be quite confusing for children.

Learning about length, mass (weight) and capacity follows a similar sequence, using these three important aspects of measuring:

Direct comparison. If you just need to know which is the smaller of two things, or whether they are the same size, the simplest way to find out is often to use direct comparison. If you want to know which skipping rope is longer, you can lay them out next to each other (making sure they are aligned at one end) to compare. If you want to know which box of beads is heavier, you could try lifting each box in turn; or if the difference is not enough to judge by feel, then you can put them on each side of a balance. If you want to find out which of two empty shampoo bottles would hold more, you can often tell by appearance, but if the appearance is misleading, you can fill the one you think is smaller, and see if the other one will hold all that, plus more. Direct comparison of two items can be extended to putting three or more items in order of size.

Using non-standard units. Sometimes, direct comparison is not sufficient or convenient. Then it becomes necessary to use either uniform non-standard units, or standard units, to measure.

The non-standard units that most adults use when measuring length are convenient human ones, such as a hand span, or the length of a foot or a stride. In everyday life, non-standard units of other sorts (such as matchsticks or cubes) are not normally used, but these can help children to see how a system of measurement works, as you can, for example, measure how many cubes high your chair seat is.

Pages 48 and 49 provide further information and activities on mass.

Using standard units. Standard units are used when more accurate measurements are needed. Centimetres and metres are the most useful ones to concentrate on for length, while millilitres and litres should be learned for capacity, and grams and kilograms for mass.

Shape and space

Here are four ways in which low-attaining children's work in shape and space can be supported.

Support the learning of new vocabulary. Make sure children are hearing new words regularly and that they have frequent opportunities to use them themselves. Check for over- or under-generalisation of new words (for example, children may use 'circle' to mean any curved shape, or restrict their use of 'square' to mean only those that are drawn parallel to the top and bottom of the page).

Improve observational skills. Use general activities where looking for similarities and differences is important, such as pairs games, dominoes and jigsaws. Find ways to help children concentrate on detailed observation through sketching, model making, and describing things.

Improve technical skills. Or find ways around shortcomings. For example, think about the drawing equipment you provide, and whether it is easy to use.

Increase children's confidence. Provide peer support. Working with a partner is much less worrying than working on your own. Encourage children to watch what others do, and to copy each other's good examples. For example, many children's skill at using construction materials is enhanced enormously by spending time copying other children's models; they then become more confident about experimenting for themselves. Similarly, children can usefully copy geometric designs and patterns that others have created, before making up designs of their own.

Pages 50 and 51 offer further information and activities on pattern making.

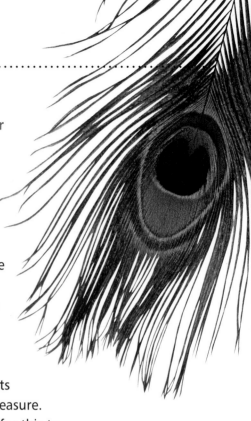

Mass

Most people (adults and children) find it quite difficult to judge how much something weighs and are generally better at estimating length than mass (weight). This is partly because people usually have more experience of measuring in centimetres or metres than of measuring in grams or kilograms.

As when learning other systems of measurement, children's work in measuring mass will go through three broad stages. The first of these is to concentrate on a *direct comparison* of two (and then more) objects, and develop the vocabulary needed to talk about them.

Next, when children start to look at measurements that cannot easily be compared directly (for example, to compare the weights of three or more objects), they can use *non-standard units* to measure. (Non-standard units do, of course, have to be of a uniform size for this to work. Plastic or wooden cubes are commonly used.)

The third stage is to start using *standard units* – the measuring systems that people invented and agreed upon to make comparisons and record-keeping easier and more accurate. The metric system of standard units for mass uses grams and kilograms.

Children will feel more confident about any system of measurement if they are familiar with key quantities. If they are not yet confident with numbers above 100, they can begin by concentrating on objects that weigh up to 100g, especially to the nearest 10g. The other main unit of mass they should become familiar with is the kilogram.

Big bags, little bags

● Use two shoe bags, two drawstring sponge bags and a variety of objects for a range of activities.

● Put some soft toys in one shoe bag, and some books in the other. Which bag is heavier?

● Put things in each little bag. Which bag is lighter? Is it easy to tell?

● Ask a child to fill a big bag and a little one, so that the big bag is *lighter* than the little bag. Many low-attaining children will initially think that this is impossible!

● Check that children understand how a balance works before you use non-standard or standard weights.

In the first picture, the two bags weigh the *same*, so the balance is level. Which bag is heavier in the second picture?

Carry a gram or a kilogram

Find something that weighs a gram (perhaps a plastic cube, such as a Centicube) and something that weighs a kilogram (a small bag of potatoes, or a big bag of pasta). Ask a child to carry the gram around for five minutes, then carry the kilogram around for five minutes. Then ask: 'How many grams do you think are the same as a kilogram? 10? 100? 1000?'

Centicube weighing

Count how many cubes (grams) it takes to balance a pair of scissors, or a pen, or a pencil sharpener. Ask the children to draw and write about what they find out.

Explain the abbreviations:

g is for gram or grams.

kg is for kilogram or kilograms.

Letter scales

Use a letter scale to weigh items under 100g to the nearest 10g. Check that children understand, for example, that the unlabelled mark between 20 and 40 must be 30g.

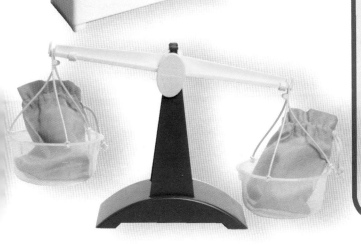

Maths you can eat!

- There is a photocopiable recipe for flapjack on page 60.

- Look for other recipes where you need to weigh 100 grams!

- Most children enjoy cooking, but few at this age will have helped to weigh ingredients. Reading the dial on ordinary kitchen scales is quite difficult, but 'diet' scales, which are labelled in smaller steps, may be easier for children to use.

Pattern making

One of the most important ways to help children improve their work in shape and space is to improve their observational skills.

Draw their attention to things around them – natural shapes and patterns as well as those created by humans. Encourage them to talk about what they can see.

Children need as wide a vocabulary as possible to be able to think and talk about shape and space. Even learning one new word can take quite a long time, particularly if the word describes a mathematical idea that is new to the child. For children to acquire a complete understanding of a new term, they need to hear the word used frequently, say it out loud as often as possible, and use it to describe or explain things so an adult can check they have fully understood it.

Describing and analysing other people's patterns, then copying patterns or inventing their own, gives children plenty of opportunities to use a wide range of mathematical vocabulary. Pattern making also helps them to develop their technical skills as they use stencils, rulers, scissors and other drawing equipment.

Drawing circles

Use a safety compass (not a traditional pair of compasses) to draw circles. These flat plastic compasses are even easier to use if children rest their work on a notepad or a magazine.

Make patterns with circles of different sizes, or all the same size.

Using stencils

Use plastic stencils or templates to draw patterns. Children usually find it easier to draw *inside* a shape than to draw *around* it.

Children can produce simple but effective patterns very easily with plastic stencils. Make sure, though, that they do not inadvertently get the impression, for example, that all hexagons are like this:

Make sure you include irregular hexagons in the examples you use for pattern making, and on displays.

Use the photocopiable sheet on page 61 for spelling practice of four useful shape names: circle, triangle, square and hexagon.

Printing

Use rubber stamps or sponge shapes to print patterns with an inkpad or with paint.

Make a frieze by turning a rubber stamp half a turn each time you print it.

Special papers

Experiment with square and triangular spotty paper, and with centimetre-squared paper. Children can draw patterns freehand, or use a 15cm bevelled ruler (because it is easier to move about than a large ruler) to draw their straight lines. Can they also draw triangles, squares, rectangles and hexagons?

See page 13 in text.

Bus counting cards

Print three copies onto card to make six counting cards.
Colour the buses in.

Extra Help in **Maths**
Ages 7–9 NC Level 2 Scottish Level B

SCHOLASTIC
PHOTOCOPIABLE

See page 13 in text.

Spider counting cards

Print three copies onto card to make six counting cards.

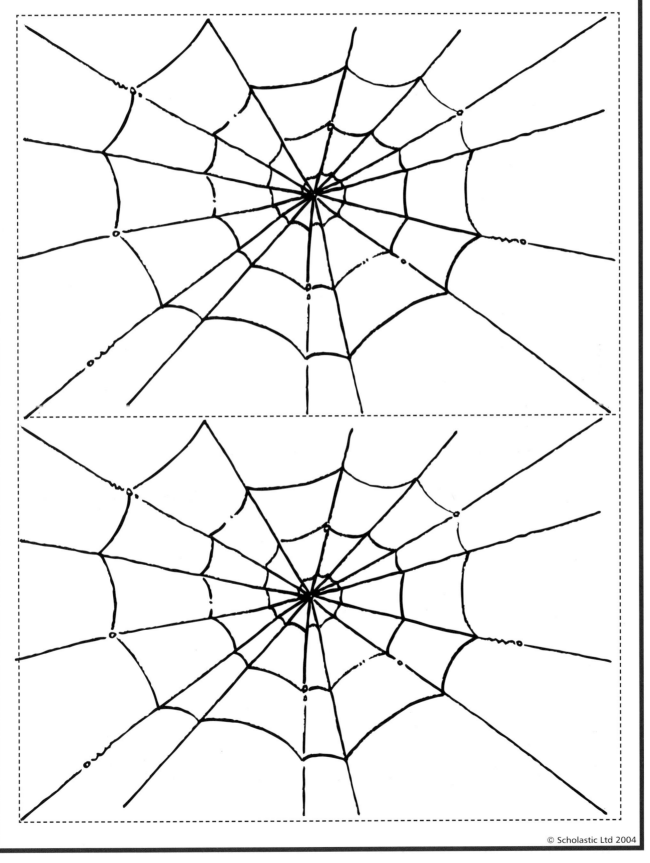

counting

Extra Help in **Maths**
Ages 7–9 NC Level 2 Scottish Level B

See page 14
in text.

counting

Letter to parents and carers

Stick your school's letterhead here.

Can you help us collect things to count?

We need:

old keys

shampoo bottle tops

postcards

toy cars

train tickets

stamps

buttons

seashells

badges

old coins

and anything else that would be interesting to count.

Thank you!

Extra Help in Maths
Ages 7–9 NC Level 2 Scottish Level B

SCHOLASTIC
PHOTOCOPIABLE

See pages 16, 17, 31 and 35 in text.

Place value cards to 99

Photocopy this sheet onto card.
Cut it up to make 18 place value cards with 'arrow' ends.

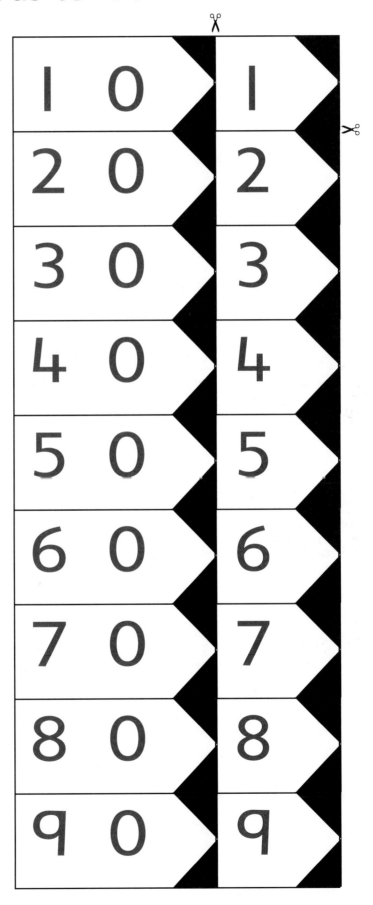

© Scholastic Ltd 2004

Extra Help in **Maths**
Ages 7–9 NC Level 2 Scottish Level B

55

counting

Name _____ Date _____

counting

Check your handwriting

How many things are in each box?
Write 0, 1, 2, 3, 4, 5, 6, 7, 8 or 9.

Which numbers do you write neatly? (✗ or ✓)

0	1	2	3	4	5	6	7	8	9

© Scholastic Ltd 2004

Extra Help in **Maths**
Ages 7–9 NC Level 2 Scottish Level B

Loop board game

Photocopy this sheet onto card or paper.

Enlarge it to A3 if you wish.

Use it to make your own loop board games.

First to

You need a dice, a counter each, and lots of objects to collect.

See page 23, 31 and 33 in text.

counting

Hundred square

Photocopy this sheet onto card.
It can also be enlarged if you wish.

1	2	3	4	5	6	7	8	9	10
11	12	13	14	15	16	17	18	19	20
21	22	23	24	25	26	27	28	29	30
31	32	33	34	35	36	37	38	39	40
41	42	43	44	45	46	47	48	49	50
51	52	53	54	55	56	57	58	59	60
61	62	63	64	65	66	67	68	69	70
71	72	73	74	75	76	77	78	79	80
81	82	83	84	85	86	87	88	89	90
91	92	93	94	95	96	97	98	99	100

Extra Help in Maths
Ages 7–9 NC Level 2 Scottish Level B

Flip-ups

Photocopy this sheet onto paper. Enlarge it to A3 if you wish.

Make this flip-up to see how they work.

Use this one to make your own flip-up.

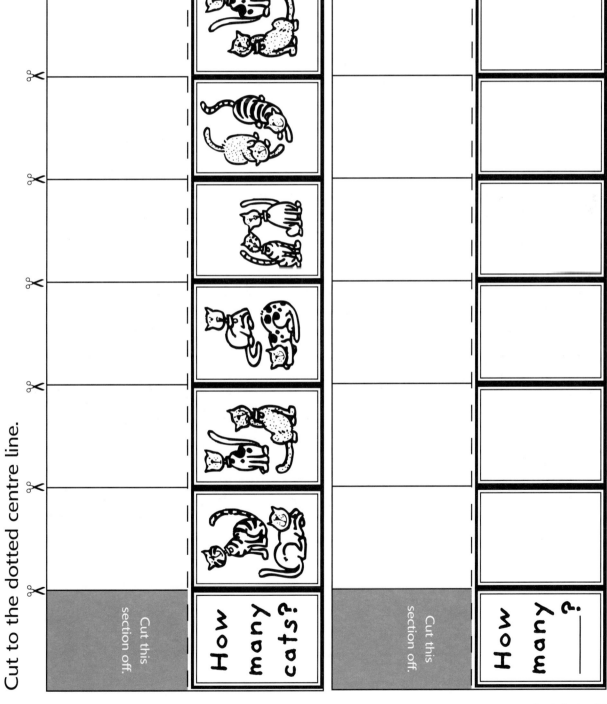

Cut to the dotted centre line.

Cut this section off.

How many cats?

Cut this section off.

How many _____?

See page 49 in text.

How to make flapjack

1. Weigh out:

100g soft margarine

100g sugar

2. Mix them together.

3. Add 100g quick oats and 50g flour. (Plain flour works best.)

Mix them into the margarine and sugar.

4. If you like, add 10–20g of sultanas and mix them in.

5. Grease a small baking tray and press the mixture into it.

6. Bake at 150°C, Gas Mark 2, or 300°F, for 20 minutes.

7. Leave to cool, then cut into squares.

© Scholastic Ltd 2004

Extra Help in **Maths**
Ages 7–9 NC Level 2 Scottish Level B

See page 51 in text.

Name _____ Date _____

Shape spellings

Copy each spelling.

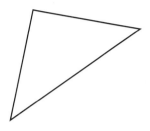 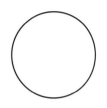  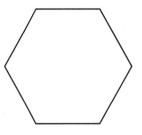

triangle   circle   square   hexagon

_____   _____   _____   _____

Write the name of each shape.

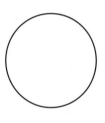  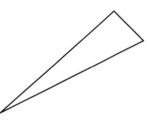 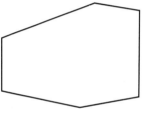

_____   _____   _____   _____

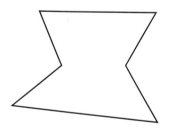  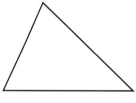

_____   _____   _____   _____

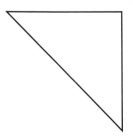 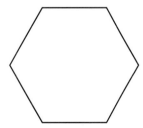 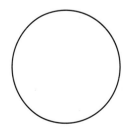

_____   _____   _____   _____

© Scholastic Ltd 2004

shape and space

Extra Help in **Maths**
Ages 7–9 NC Level 2 Scottish Level B

Summary of objectives

			Count reliably up to 100 objects including by grouping them: for example, in tens, then in fives or twos.	Read and write whole numbers to at least 100.	Order whole numbers to at least 100, and position them on a number line and 100 square.	Within the range 0 to 30, say the number that is 1 or 10 more or less than any given number.	Know what each digit in a two-digit number represents, including 0 as a place holder, and partition two-digit numbers into a multiple of ten and ones (TU).	Describe and extend simple number sequences: count on or back in ones or tens, starting from any two-digit number.	Recognise odd and even numbers to at least 30.	Use and begin to read the vocabulary of estimation and approximation.	Understand the operation of addition, and of subtraction (as 'take away', 'difference' and 'how many more to make'), and use the related vocabulary.
number	Counting games	12	●	●		○					
	Counting library	14	●	●						●	
	Reading and writing numbers to 100	16	○	●							
	Counting in tens and ones	18	●	●		●	●	●			
	Board games	20	●	●	○	○					
	Making one hundred	22	●	●	●						
	Numbers in order	24	○	●	●	●		○	●		
calculations	Practical problems	28	○	○							
	Adding with tens and ones	30	●	●	●	●	●	●			
	Subtraction	32	●	●	●	●	●	●			
	Learning number facts	34	○	○		●					
	Using the number line	36	●	●	●	●	●	●			
	Early multiplication and division	38	○					●			
	Money	40	●	●			●	○			
	Role play and money	42	●	●			○			●	
	Sums in words	44	○	●						○	
measures, shape and space	Mass	48	○	○						●	
	Pattern making	50									

numbers and the number system

The teaching and learning objectives in this book are matched to the National Curriculum's Attainment Targets for Mathematics at Level 2:

Attainment target 1:
using and applying mathematics

Attainment target 2:
number and algebra

Attainment target 3:
shape, space and measures

Details on the precise content of these attainment targets can be found on pages 9, 11 and 13 of the leaflet at the back of the National Curriculum handbook, and on the National Curriculum website at www.nc.uk.net/nc/contents/ma--2-att.html

objectives

Summary of teaching and learning objectives, matched to _The National Numeracy Strategy_ (England), _Framework for Teaching Mathematics from Reception to Year 6_. All at Level 2 of the National Curriculum.

...facts for each number to at least 10.	Use knowledge that addition can be done in any order to do mental calculations more efficiently.	Understand that subtraction is the inverse of addition (subtraction reverses addition).	Understand the operation of multiplication as repeated addition or as describing an array.	Know and use halving as the inverse of doubling.	Choose and use appropriate operations and efficient calculation strategies to solve problems, explaining how the problem was solved.	Solve mathematical problems or puzzles, recognise simple patterns and relationships, generalise and predict. Suggest extensions by asking 'What if...?' or 'What could I try next?'	Recognise all coins and begin to use £.p notation for money (for example, know that £4.65 indicates £4 and 65p). Find totals, give change, and work out which coins to pay.	Understand and use the vocabulary related to length, mass and capacity.	Compare two lengths, masses or capacities by direct comparison; extend to more than two. Measure using uniform non-standard units or standard units.	Use the mathematical names for common 3-D and 2-D shapes, including the cube, cuboid, sphere, cylinder, cone..., circle, triangle, square, rectangle...	Make and describe shapes, pictures and patterns using, for example, templates, pinboard and elastic bands, squared paper, a programmable robot...	Make whole turns and half turns. Use one or more shapes to make, describe and continue repeating patterns.
						●						
						●						
						●						
						●						
					●	●						
						●						
						●						
○	○	●			●	●						
	●				●	●						
		●			●	●						
●	●	●				●						
	●				●							
			●	●	●	●						
	○	○			●	●	●					
	○	○	●		●	●	●					
○	●	●	●		●	●	○					
						●		●	●			
						●				●	●	●

| **calculations** | | | | | **solving problems** | | | **measures, shape and space** | | | | |

● main focus   ○ also useful

Extra Help in **Maths**
Ages 7–9 NC Level 2 Scottish Level B

63

Summary of objectives

Summary of teaching and learning objectives, matched to *Curriculum and Assessment in Scotland, National Guidelines, Mathematics 5–14*. All at Level B.

	shape, space and measures		calculations									numbers and the number system						
	Pattern making	Mass	Sums in words	Role play and money	Money	Early multiplication and division	Using the number line	Learning number facts	Subtraction	Adding with tens and ones	Practical problems	Numbers in order	Making one hundred	Board games	Counting in tens and ones	Reading and writing numbers to 100	Counting library	Counting games
	50	48	44	42	40	38	36	34	32	30	28	24	22	20	18	16	14	12
Problem solving and enquiry	●	●	●	●	●	●	●	●	●	●	●	●	●	●	●	●	●	●
Number, money and measurement																		
Range and type of numbers: Whole numbers up to 100 (count, order, read and write).		O	O	●	●	O	●	O	●	●	●	●	●	●	●	●	●	●
Money: Use coins up to £1 including exchange.				●	●													
Add and subtract: Mentally for numbers 0 to 20; without a calculator for 2-digit numbers; in applications in number, measurement and money.			●	●	●	O	●	●	●	●	●		●					
Round numbers: Round 2-digit whole numbers to the nearest ten.		●	O	●													●	
Patterns and sequences: Work with patterns and sequences: even and odd numbers; whole number sequences within 100; more complex sequences with shapes.	●					O	●	●				●	●	●	●			
Measure and estimate: Measure in easily handled standard units. Read scales on measuring devices to the nearest graduation.	O	●																
Shape, position and movement																		
Range of shapes: Collect, discuss, make and use 3-D and 2-D shapes.	●	O																

● main focus   O also use